THE BROKEN KEY

KEY

Restoration Of My Life Played
On A Broken Key

BY
GARY DIGGS

FOREWORD

I've never written a foreword as effortlessly as this one. *The Broken Key* checks all the boxes when illuminating the journey of not only a preacher's kid but of anybody who has grown up in the church. There is no doubt that the reader will easily find themselves appearing in this well-written and timeless piece of literature.

Thank you, Mr. Diggs, for this homerun. *—Dr. Lonnie Hunter*

I'm excited for his new book *The Broken Key*, and I know that it will be a blessing to anyone who reads it with a heart to grow and to serve God with their gifts while grappling with their own brokenness and dysfunction.

—Sam Towns, Hobart, Australia

I first met Gary when he and the team came to minister at our church in Newcastle, Australia, some fifteen years ago. He was so encouraging, and it was an honor to sing with him as he played and ministered. We have since remained friends and I've watched Gary from afar remain steadfast and encouraging while continuing to be a worshipper, especially through the hills and valleys of life! I have no doubt this book will bring freedom and release as he shares his heart around the journey of His life.

—*Amanda Batterham, Newcastle, Australia*

GARY DIGGS, MUSICIAN/SONGWRITER

A native of Camden, New Jersey, this seasoned musician has garnered a reputation for writing and producing warm, heartfelt, and infectious songs that engage the heart. He coins his style of music as soulful, and credits the favor of God and hard work with affording him national and international notoriety in the music business. Gary's musical gift has allowed him to work with a range of noteworthy talents like Bishop David G. Evans, former President Bill Clinton, the National Basketball Association's (NBA) Allen Iverson, the late Edwin Hawkins, Lonnie Hunter, Earnest Pugh, Micah Stampley, and others.

Gary started his early teenage years as a church organist at Emmanuel United Pentecostal Church in Camden, New Jersey, which his parents, the late Bishop Sherman Sr. and Mother Dorothy Diggs, founded in 1968. He has traveled the world and has written and produced songs that have scored both Billboard's Gospel Top Charts and Stellar Nominations.

Gary is the owner of several life-impacting ministries: *D'Garia Music Group, Called To Refresh, Cover Me Summit* (an event to empower, challenge, produce, and financially support students as they return to school in September), L'NIS (Life Now Is Sweet Senior Care), The Conversation (Facebook Live), and the author of *The Broken Key.*

He can be reached at P.O. Box 1672, Merchantville, NJ 08109 or Email: gary_diggs@yahoo.com

Facebook: Gary Diggs / Instagram: garyediggs / Website: www.garyediggs.com

CONTENTS

CONTENTS

CHAPTER 1

From Karate to Piano

S omewhere between the ages of three and five, I tagged along with my older brother David to his piano lessons. While there, I watched karate until he was done. One day, after hearing the repetitions of the melody from the piano, it stuck in my head. Back at home, I jumped on the piano and began to play what I heard at his lesson. My oldest brother, Sherman Jr., stopped playing football and ran inside the house to see what the screaming and commotion were about. To his surprise, along with that of Mom, David, and my older two sisters Carolyn and Sharon, their baby brother Doonky was playing what I heard: *How I Got Over.* Doonky is my nickname, given at my birth by my siblings. Growing up in a musical family, where everyone played an instrument, creative writing was always in motion. When I cried excessively, Mom jumped on the piano and my siblings started singing one of two songs they had made up about Doonky.

(Proverbs 22:6) "Train up a child in the way he should go: and when he is old, he will not depart from it."

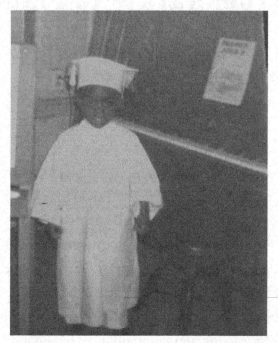

CHAPTER 2

The Discovery Gone Bad

The news is now out, who's that Diggs boy playing the piano and his feet can't even reach the pedals yet? After many guest appearances at schools, church events, and some local TV shows, national offers were starting to pour in. One day, a promoter who was getting me several engagements met with my parents and said, "You have something special in Gary, and I need to take him to California."

Mom said, "Well, we need to pray and further discuss with an attorney before we sign and make any haste decisions."

The promoter said, "Well you need to act fast, because we can make a lot of money off him now and, not to mention, "I did discover him."

Those who knew my mom, know she was not the one to play with. She immediately told the promoter, "You did no such thing," this is an anointing God has placed on him and we will not allow you or anyone else to use his gift for their own gain. A few months later we learned this promoter was a scam and was out to use me.

(John 10:10) "The thief comes only to steal and kill and destroy. I came that they may have life and have it abundantly."

CHAPTER 3

Hustled

B y age twelve, I was playing fluently and was being called to accompany singers. Sometime, I would receive twenty-five or fifty dollars, and even had offerings raised for me. But there's always a hustler in church clothes. One time a singer just paid for my dinner after a concert and said, "Doc you were killing and thank you for playing for me. One day I'll be able to pay you." He didn't know that I saw the deacon hand him an envelope full of cash.

As a teenager, I was starting to miss some school days because I was either flying out on Friday mornings or returning

Monday evenings to fulfill engagements. One day we get a call for my first organ recording session with a producer who saw me play at a concert. After all the talk about his production credits and all he planned to do for me, he was even willing to work around my schoolwork. My parents agreed to take me to a ten p.m. studio recording session. Once the session was over and we left somewhere around three a.m., the producer promised to come past the house after the banks opened to bring my pay. Of course, back then there were no Cash Apps and no ATM Machines. Needless to say, he got his recordings and I never got paid or heard back from him again.

(Romans 12:17) "Repay no one evil for evil, but give thought to do what is honorable in the sight of all."

CHAPTER 4

The Grocery Cart

In November 1986, I was seventeen years old and in my high school's co-op program. My job was gathering grocery carts at Pathmark. A few hours into my work while gathering carts in the frigid cold, I heard my name called over the loudspeakers, "Gary Diggs, come to the registers for customer assistance." It was the day before Thanksgiving, busy, cold, and snowy outside. I was just glad to get back inside for some heat. I got to the cash register and there stood a little lady, bundled up with a hat over her head hiding her face. The customer winked at me as I assisted her to the car with her groceries.

To my surprise, it was my mom. She said, "Boy it's too cold out here and you are going to mess up your hands." She proceeded to say, "I spoke with someone who will give you a desk job." Without hesitation, I jumped in the car and left with her. Ironically, the Equifax Services Paintwork building I worked in at age seventeen for three years was down the street from Bethany Baptist Church where I've been working at for the past 18 years.

(Psalm 119:105) "Thy word is a lamp unto
my feet, a light unto my path."

CHAPTER 5

Pen of a Ready Writer

I played for my high school's gospel choir and grew irresponsible, being late or not showing up for rehearsals as my popularity begin to set in. One day during a school performance, to my surprise, the choir director benched me and the choir sung without music to a full audience of faculty and students. I was highly embarrassed in front of my peers. Later that day, the director called me into the auditorium and explained that God gives us the talent but we're responsible to nurture it. The very next day, I went to the school's band teacher and asked permission to play the piano. He let me practice in the music room everyday on my lunch and during study hall periods. It was there that I wrote *Goin' Back*, which would a few years later in 1993 hit the Billboard Top Gospel Charts for more than thirty-three weeks with Edwin Hawkins Tri-State Mass Choir, a community choir formed by my uncle, the late James A. Viner. I did not know that God had anointed me and made my tongue the pen of a ready writer. After the success of that song, I began to write, play, and produce other songs for them, along with other gospel recording artists. I was writing, but I didn't know anything about writer and publishing agreements until years later. Shame on those who do not teach inexperienced songwriters about copyrights and royalties. God has redeemed the time. (Isaiah 52:12) The glory of the Lord shall be thy reward.

The Tri-State Mass Choir celebrated thirty years in music ministry with a live DVD recording on September 12, 2015, in Camden, New Jersey, performed in front of a sold-out audience. In honor of my late uncle James A. Viner, we changed the name to JV's Tri-State Reunion Choir.

(Psalm 45:1) "My heart is inditing a good matter: I speak of the things which I have made touching the king: my tongue is the pen of a ready writer."

CHAPTER 6

The Car Accident

I n April 1987, my older brother David and I were in a bad car accident after leaving a spring concert. It was a Saturday evening, and Mom said, "I think you should come straight home afterward," because I had a full schedule the next day.

Being young and liking the girls, I said "I won't be out late, ignored her suggestion, and rushed on to the social gathering." Just before midnight, on our way home on Route 676, someone cut across the lane and our car spun out of control. I thought life was over. The police and David applied pressure on my face with a towel until the EMTs arrived. I could hear David repeatedly scream "Oh, God," and the policeman say they thought I lost the eye because of all the blood. I was rushed to Wills Eye Hospital in Philadelphia only to find out that just my eyelids were split. Thank you Jesus! Although I missed several weeks of school, I did march and graduate.

To The Class of 2020:

COVID-19 has interrupted some things, but not your futures!

(Jeremiah 29:11) "For I know the thoughts that I think toward you, saith the Lord, thoughts of peace, and not of evil, to give you an expected end."

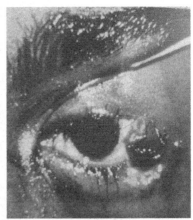
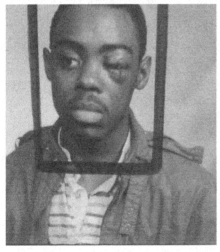

CHAPTER 7

Immaturity—The Costly Mistake

By then I was out of high school and ditched college to hit the road making money. I was traveling and was booked every weekend. I promised my parents to buy them a big house, fancy cars, and so on. For the first time, I was on the road without my parents' supervision. My song *Goin Back* was soaring on the gospel billboard charts and the Tri-State Mass Choir was on tour, scheduled to perform at a huge concert. We arrived the day before and, to my surprise, I saw the Who's Who of Gospel Music. I was overwhelmed at the fact that so many gospel recording artists I had grown up listening to and had seen on TV were actually in the lobby of this hotel. My uncle James, who was a major influence on my music journey, handed me my hotel room key and gave me the itinerary. So I looked around and froze, star struck. I said to him, "I'm not coming out of my room until it's time to check out."

Being immature and mouthy, I said a few not-so-nice words out of fear and he said, "We've paid your expenses and fee and you will play tomorrow night even if I have to drag you on stage." My uncle was no pushover.

I said thank you to be polite, but in my mind, I was not coming out of my room until it was time to check out. The next morning there was a loud knock on my hotel door. I thought it was room service, but no, it was my mom.

She was furious and said, "What's wrong with you? I had to catch a flight out of Philadelphia to get here this morning." So we talked and she said, "Did someone touch you?"

I said, "No, ma'am."

She said, "Did someone look at you or say something out of the way?"

I said, "No, ma'am." I said, "Mom I'm nervous and scared."

She said, "Gary, you are here to spread the gospel. These are people who put their pants on one leg at a time. Your assignment is for the lost and to minister to all crowd sizes with the love and grace of God."

That was a costly mistake and could have damaged my career at that time.

Mom said, "And another thing, you will apologize to your uncle, then prepare to minister tonight and play unto the Lord." I called my uncle, apologized, and got ready for the concert. Yes, the Lord blessed us and we got other dates from that night. My pastor, Bishop David G. Evans, once told me you have to learn how to preach a steady gospel on a rocky boat.

(Psalm 27:13) "I had fainted, unless I had believed to see the goodness of the Lord in the land of the living."

CHAPTER 8:

Thread the Needle

M y mom was a wife, mother, grandmother, aunt, sister, first lady of our church, and she was also contracted as a seamstress for various retail stores and private clients. However, as she got older, her weakened eyesight wouldn't allow her to thread needles. Many times in the middle of my favorite tv show or street football game, she yelled out, "Gary, come here." You can only imagine my frustration at having to stop what I was doing, but Mom only had to call my name one time or else. She needed my eyes to thread her needle, than I could return to my activities.

Too often we assume we have forever with love ones and put off phone calls, text, and even visits with that special some-one. Life is but a fleeting moment, be sure to share many of those with loves ones. Oh, what I would do to be able to thread her needle again. Cherish the time with your love ones.

(Exodus 20:12) "Honour thy father and thy mother: that thy days may be long upon the land which the Lord thy God giveth thee."

CHAPTER 9

Mom Said Goodbye, but Never Left

As a family, we ate dinner together every day once Dad got home from the Pepsi-Cola Bottling Company where he worked. I have so many great memories of living on Vine Street. Our neighbors were one big family. There was no talk of electronics, we played in the water from the fire hydrant, we played football, stickball, tag, hide and go seek, king, doorbell dixie, and basketball with a milk crate cut out at the bottom and nailed to a utility pole. We played for hours, and it seemed like time stood still. But when I saw the church van turn the corner, that was my signal that Dad was home and it was time for dinner. As I stated earlier, my parents only had to call my name one time.

Growing up in such a God-loving home with both parents, four siblings, and a couple of dogs—Keena and Gigi— the world seemed perfect to me. All I knew was a good life at home, walking to school, playing with my friends, and I went to church it seemed like every evening. I couldn't go to house parties, couldn't stay overnight at friends' homes, I had to be on my own porch by sundown, and could only listen to gospel music in the house. Even now, I enjoy only gospel and occasionally classical and jazz.

As life was moving forward, my siblings were getting married and moving out, so what was already a small home with seven people became larger now with just Dad, Mom, and me. I finally had my own room, no more sharing bathwater with my older brother David. We lived on a very tight budget, but my parents put much wisdom, love, domestic skills, and work ethic inside of us to ensure we understood life outside of Vine Street. They reminded us daily to give God our best, to take Him everywhere we went, and to remain humbled with all accomplishments.

It was dinnertime, and once again Mom always prepared a great meal. I can remember at times Mom left the kitchen while we were eating, not knowing that there was not always enough food. She wanted to make sure we all got plenty to eat. As she returned to the kitchen to clear place settings, she grabbed the cold food to make herself a plate.

In 1992, Mom made an announcement at dinner that she had been diagnosed with pancreatic cancer and the chances of a cure were slim to none. The news really didn't bother me, because she was super Mom and I had seen her lay hands on the sick and they recovered, I watched her jump in front of a guy holding a gun and he put it away, I remember she had moles all over her body and anointed herself with oil than took a bath and they all fell off. Even at our church, I had seen countless miracles after miracles. I saw a church member pronounced dead in the hospital and minutes later she sat up and said, "I'm still here." I saw one member scheduled for emergency open-heart surgery and the doctor said, "Hold up, I need one more x-ray before I cut on her," and the test results came back negative. Both ladies are alive today. I watched people come in our church drunk, passed out on the bench. My parents told the ushers leave them alone, and they sobered up and years later became leaders at the ministry.

Pancreatic cancer was another excuse for God to move. However, a few months after this news, Mom began losing weight and strength and, for the first time in my life, she began to miss weekly church services. I was watching my super mom, the lady with style, class, elegance, strength, humility, and yes, my mommy, Mother Dorothy Elizabeth Diggs, who stepped out weekly in tailored, designer dresses she made with matching accessories. Now I was seeing her lay in bed with a housecoat and down to ninety pounds, even writing it brings me to tears. She laid there and sang to my older sister Sharon and I, *I Saw The Light* and we just cried and said, "Mom, you gonna be alright."

She stopped us and said, "If you can take it you can make it. I need y'all to hold on, keep God first, stay together, and remember that no good thing will God withhold from you if you walk up right before Him." Mom told me, "My job is done and you are now equipped." She said, "Gary, you know more than how to just make money and babies. You can cook, clean, shop for yourself, sew on buttons, and stitch up a hole." My oldest sister, Carolyn, flew back into the country to be with Dad, Sherman, Sharon, David, and me as we watched Mom blow us a kiss on August 11, 1993. She said goodbye, but her spirit never left.

(Psalm 61:2) "From the end of the earth I will
cry to You, when my heart is overwhelmed;
lead me to the rock that is higher than I."

CHAPTER 10

Dad, Can We Play Catch?

L ike any child, you run to greet your parents when they get in from work. Dad was an honorable, soft-spoken, loving, great man of God. Mom did the spankings, but Dad did the "Let's take a car ride and talk about it." He talked in a soft voice until you wished he would have just spanked you. He stood six foot, three inches tall with thirty-eight-inch-long arms. I asked, "Dad, how much do you love me?"

He replied by stretching his arms out, and said, "This much."

I said, "Wow, that's a lot of love."

Dad was always full of surprises and gifts for us. It could be apples, a bike, or half a sandwich he had at lunch with his co-worker Barry Mazzio. Dad worked all day and pastored a growing church. As a kid, I didn't understand why he didn't always have time to play catch. I watched him rush in from work, kiss Mom, grab a quick bite of dinner, change clothes, and head to church. He didn't like to be late, so at times he just went straight to church and preached and taught in his Pepsi uniform. I remember trying to build a doghouse for my German Shepherd Keena.

I asked Dad for help, and he said, "Gary, I'll help you over the weekend because I have to get to church."

Being somewhat spoiled, I sat on the backyard steps and cried loud enough for Mom to hear and she told Dad, "At least show him what to do so he doesn't hurt himself or cut his fingers off fooling with those tools."

Dad, in his suit and tie, grabbed the saw, cut the wood, and nailed the boards together so fast that he didn't even get my input. So he said, "Is this okay?

I said, "No, Sir, you made the doghouse with a flat roof, I want a big doghouse with a triangle-shaped roof." So for years, I felt the church was taking him away from me. As a child, I said that when I get older and have children, I will never go to church and I will never let church be in my relationship.

As I got older, I begin to understand and realized that Dad really loved me and he had his assignment as husband, father of five, pastor, and Pepsi. I was appointed minister of music in 1986, and began to work with Dad in ministry and run with his vision for the ministry. And I finally began to understand he was never neglecting me as his son. He was actually teaching me independence as a man.

Dad was always teaching with illustrations. One day he handed me some money, he said, "Put this money in your left front pocket, than grab it with your right hand."

I said, "That's difficult."

He said, "Exactly." He was teaching me, that making money is a task, so save as much as possible. When you want something use your right hand, but when you need something use your left hand to grab the money to pay for it. Basically, think before spending and be a good steward. We did get to rebuild the doghouse and added some shingles on the roof.

(John 3:35) "The Father loves the Son and has given all things into his hand."

CHAPTER 11

I'm Grown, Or So I Thought

By age twenty-three, I had already traveled internationally, I had money in my pockets, great credit, new cars, was used to eating in the best of restaurants, and was wearing designer, tailored suits. Mom had died, so things had begun to privately fall apart in my life because I had not dealt with her passing. I began to privately live recklessly with my money and to add to my mess, I got married with no plans, no discipline, and no idea of the responsibilities. I had to reschedule the wedding twice because by then I was broke and needed the money I got from performing. I got married November 19, 1994, and nine months later I was holding our baby girl, named Destiny Garia Diggs. My dad said, "This is serious, and you need to make some immediate decisions now that you have a family."

The math didn't make sense to take a nine to five job working forty hours a week and make three to four hundred dollars versus playing the organ for someone for forty minutes and making the same amount. However, being obedient, I got an office job with benefits in the mailroom, at eight-twenty-five an hour, then was quickly promoted to team lead, and then on to supervisor. A couple of years later, I was offered a position as area manager, which required traveling. So I was making more money than I had ever made. I bought a house, a new car, the best of clothes for my family, and we took multiple family getaways a year. Basically, I began living privately recklessly again, trying to erase the pain of my mom and now my uncle James's death.

After seven years of plenty, things began to fall apart. We had utility bills, a mortgage, car repairs, and creditors knocking and were constantly playing catch up. In previous years, all I had to do was get a few road trips to clear up everything up, but the road trips slowed down. I was in self-destruction mode. To add to my breakdown, I lost my job. So there I was, sitting there with all of these assets and no savings. I called my dad and said, "I want to die and not live anymore. I have a family and stuff that I can't take care of anymore."

He felt my pain through the phone. He said, "Bow your head," and he prayed with me and said, "Father this is my son and yes he is in a mess, but I need you to give him one of my blessings today in the name of Jesus thank God amen." He said, "I want you to be encouraged and watch God work on your behalf."

Several weeks later I was working for the U.S. Post Office, then on to Temple University, and was hired to produce music to the best-selling book *Healed Without Scars* by David G. Evans. After that project, I was able to go into music ministry full time. "Thank you, Dad, for your prayers."

(1 Corinthians 13:11) "When I was as a child, I understood as a child, I thought as a child: but when I became a man, I put away childish things."

CHAPTER 12

From Daddy, Take Care
to Daddy Daycare

Working more that sixty hours a week, with a daughter now in college, and a music-production schedule that kept me quite busy, reduced the amount of talking time with Dad. We had short conversations once a week that quickly ended with, "Daddy, take care."

Even with all of the music success, I stayed on as minister of music at my childhood church Emmanuel United Pentecostal Church in Camden, New Jersey, that he and Mom founded in 1968. Dad looked over at me with a smile as I played the organ, which gave me assurance that he was pleased with his baby boy. He often told the church, that when mom was pregnant he wanted his youngest child to be a boy because, he said, by the time he was old he would need a son to take care of him. So as I sat at the organ every first Sunday, seeing the power of God moved in the service, I would see Dad nodding his head, winking at me, and making a fist singing his signature song, *Life Now Is Sweet*.

Oh, what a blessing, I thought, *for us to be in ministry together.* By then Dad was in his eighties and not driving as much. I rarely took him to the doctor, because he was relatively healthy. I was on the road traveling and I got a call from my oldest sister, Carolyn, saying, "We all need to talk."

When big sister calls a meeting, it's urgent. She explained that Dad was diagnosed with early-stage Alzheimer's disease, so him living on his own was no longer an option. Dad stayed with Carolyn and her family during the week and with Sharon and her family on weekends. One day I was visiting Dad and told Carol, "You shouldn't have to do this when he has three sons. Let me take Dad to my home." So it went from "Daddy, take care" to Daddy day care. Oh, what a blessing to have him in my home. The daily prayers, checker games, puzzles, meals together, and his grace, wisdom, and the peace he brought there were unforgettable. I immediately apologized to him for not spending more time with him over the years and he stopped me and said, "Son, things happen, and I want you to know I really love you."

As his Alzheimer's progressed, I recall him saying, "Oh, my, I'm in bad shape, man, I don't know where I am and I need some money to get a bus back home." Then he calmed down by laying hands on himself and praying, "Help, Lord." He told me, "I trust God and I know that he has me in his hands."

Dad forgot a lot of things, but he never forgot his relationship with God. He prayed, read, and studied his bible daily. We took drives to get ice cream or just sit on my deck, and he would say, "I'm sorry man, but where are we?"

I cried internally because he was slipping away. But he would come right back with "God is good" or sing *I'm Holding my Savior's Hand.* His love for God never wavered. The bible says (1 John 2:14), "And so I say to you fathers who know the eternal God, and to you young men who are strong with God's Word in your hearts, and have won your struggle against Satan." You can imagine no expense was spared as his five children secured our father's care. He had a personal home health aide to help start his day. He had a physical therapist to exercise and work with his memory loss.

I recall his friend Deacon Robert Mitchell spending the day with Dad. When I returned from a day trip to New York he said, "Brother Gary, Bishop hasn't eaten all day and he seems to not be feeling well." This was a Wednesday, and I was due at Bible Study shortly, but without hesitation I called out of work and stayed home. My niece LaToya, her husband Alvin, and my older sister Sharon came to my house, and decided to take Dad to the hospital. Alvin carried his weak body to my car. We didn't know that would be his last night in my home.

I sat by his bed, begging God to give me more time with the man I lost so much time with in my early years. I found myself standing again around a hospital bed with my siblings watching Dad take his last breath. Our family of seven was now reduced to five. Although I have played at hundreds of funerals over the years, I'm not immune from this kind of bereavement pain.

Dad passed away on Christmas Eve, December 24, 2016. I left the hospital angry and with questions as to why didn't God answer my prayer. I was grateful for all the phone calls, texts, and social media posts filled with condolences and well wishes, however, I said I needed time off to compress this anger, now that I had lost both parents. I didn't want to bleed on the congregations and needed inner healing. The next day was Christmas morning, and I woke up with no intention of going to church, but I felt like David in second Samuel, chapter twelve, verse twenty, "He got up from the floor, washed his face and combed his hair, put on a fresh change of clothes, then went into the sanctuary and worshipped."

So I got washed, dressed, and went to my church, Bethany Baptist Church in Lindenwold, New Jersey, and got on the organ. As Bishop Evans sat there, he nodded his head at me just like my parents nodded at me over the years. I fought back the tears and played. When I got in the presence of God, all I could hear was the Lord tell me "I am well pleased with you, your parents' earthly work is done."

Death brings so many questions to the caregivers. *What could I have done differently? Should I have changed doctors?* So many thoughts and questions came to mind. The bible says in Psalm one-forty-seven, verse three, "He heals the broken-hearted and binds up their wounds." Our pain isn't hidden from God; rather, He offers us relief and healing, if we show Him our brokenness and invite Him into the pain.

CHAPTER 13

Living in the Belly
like Jonah

J onah, chapter one, verse seventeen says, "Now the Lord had prepared a great fish to swallow Jonah. And Jonah was in the belly of the fish three days and three nights."

In 2019, I awakened from a dream I was having. I could see this huge fish with a little bit of everything on the inside of its stomach. I saw successful people, homeless people, big houses, apartments, office building, and even churches. I jumped up in a cold sweat, trying to understand what was its meaning. God revealed to me that those are people who ran from Him. I said, "But they seem to be living normal lives and some seem to be doing well."

He told me there are people doing well, but not well doing. He said just imagine if they had not run from me. The revelation from the dream was that I was chasing the riches and in pursuit of the American dream, and assumed I was doing well. But to my surprise, doing well and well doing are not the same thing.

I know there was a call on my life to preach as a kid, but I ran like Jonah. He ran to a boat, I ran to music ministry, I ran to corporate life, I ran to women, I ran and stumbled over hardship. The wonderful thing about God is He will never leave you nor forsake you. I fell on my face, repented, and begged God for forgiveness for wasting while waiting as that prodigal son. God heard my cry. I'm out of the belly, back to writing, ministering, and doing workshops and for once in my life I'm living in peace.

CHAPTER 14

Stay Woke
(Don't Waste While Waiting)

T he Bible reads (2 Thessalonians 3:10), "If a man will not work, he shall not eat." After misappropriations and mismanagement of my own investments, I've made it a mission of mine to educate up-and-coming fathers, musicians, and to anyone that will listen to ensure they don't have to waste while waiting for His return. (Ephesians 5:16) "Redeeming the time, because the days are evil."

Today I run several ministries that are dear to my heart:

- Called To Refresh (April, the first Tuesday after Easter)

- Cover Me Summit—Back To School Event (September, the first Tuesday in September)

- D'Garia Music Group—Musician, Songwriter, Workshop, Author

- L'NIS (Life Now Is Sweet) Daycare for Seniors in honor of my parents, the late Bishop Sherman Sr. and Mother Dorothy Diggs) every Thursday from ten a.m. to two p.m.

- The Conversation—Facebook Live with an industry guest

- Author of *The Broken Key*

CHAPTER 15

The Broken Key

I grew up in an environment where holiness is right, look like you're saved, talk and act like you're saved, no drinking of alcohol or wine, no illegal drugs, no premarital sex, no sports on Sunday, no worldly music played in the house, where women could not wear pants in church, men had to wear ties to church, no girls in my bedroom, and all TV shows were censored. I think you get where I've been. At the time it seemed that everything other than being a Christian was fun and we were just boring holy rollers. As I mentioned a few chapters back when I thought I was grown up, the rules and doctrines, mixed with biblical truth, made me curious. So I learned to sin privately. Immaturity will cause a person with all the security, safety, and support to abandon them for riotous living. I privately spiraled out of control and struggled unnecessarily because I was in search of fun and not joy. I learned to do ministry and misery at the same time.

Shout on Sunday, mess up on Monday, clean up on Tuesday to prepare to minister Wednesday, then live right on Thursday convicted by the word I heard on Wednesday evening, mess up again on Friday, than clean up again Saturday evening for Sunday. I had enough sense not to fall around the saints because I was a preacher's kid, and getting caught or being in a compromising position would not be good for my reputation. So I learned to be sneaky and justified it by saying, *I'm not hurting anyone and I do my assignments and I'm always faithful with no questions regarding my integrity and commitment to ministry. After all, I grew up in church and I knew how to look, walk, talk, and wave my hand at the right time.* It's simply flesh on parade.

A broken key on the piano was a teaching point that changed my life. A musician once told me, "A good musician can play around a broken key, but at some point the audience will know there's a problem. But a great musician will never let the audience hear the broken key." Over forty years of traveling, I've played many keyboards, pianos, and organs, and have noticed there are no two alike. Many times, as a guest, while

I'm waiting to play, I hear musicians and they sound amazing, I then sat down to play on the very same instrument they just finished playing and immediately noticed sticking or no sustain pedals, and, to add insult to injury, I see broken keys. I wondered why it sounded so amazing while they were playing, as if nothing was wrong. It was years before it hit me that they knew their own brokenness just like I knew mine. I learned to adjust, play around the broken keys, play other octaves, and modulate if necessary. I did anything to get through this song of life. But I made a conscious decision. I was tired of operating wounded and playing on broken keys. I needed peace. I called the piano tuner, I mean I called on Jesus and asked the savior to forgive and wash me in the blood of the lamb. The blood will never lose its power. Oh, what joy that is in my soul now that my broken key is repaired.

Yes, this preacher's kid hit bad notes at times in my recording session called life, but the great producer and engineer, God himself deletes and allows me to overdub and play the melody of my day again. (Lamentations 3:22) "Through the Lord's mercies we are not consumed, Because His compassions fail not."

So all the church language, rules, doctrine, and biblical teaching I've learned over the years, I now understand was never meant to make me bitter but better. The church is the house of God, the bride, a place of reverence, a sanctified place, and a shelter from the storm. So we honor the church with our best. I recall when I was younger, people would stop cussing and even hide their cigarettes as they walked pass the church as respect unto the Lord. Just as we have rules in our homes, on our jobs, and in the public establishments, how much more should we honor the house of God?

I released a song in 2019, *I Can U Can*, that deals with so many mistakes I made, but faith not feelings keep me pressing forward. To my worship leaders, if we are not careful we will bleed on our audience with our own broken keys. Be healed, set free and delivered, and allow God over your life.

(1 John 1:9) "If we confess our sins, he is faithful and just to forgive us our sins, and to cleanse us from all unrighteousness."

Be Blessed and a Blessing Today!

THANK YOU

Dedicated to my parents: The late Bishop Sherman Senior and Mother Dorothy E. Diggs

Doria E. Diggs; Destiny Diggs; Carolyn (Garland) Kinard family; Sherman (Pamela) Diggs, Jr. family; Sharon (Charles) Anfield family; David (Roslyn) Diggs family; James A. Viner; Bishop David G. Evans; Alex Ingram; Lonnie Hunter; Jamie (Chelsey) Williams; Bethany Baptist Church family; Emmanuel United Pentecostal Church family; Fred Blain; Richard Tubbs Smith, Jr.; Eugene (Delphine) Martin; Derrick Hodge; Parris Bowens; Jerod Howard, Cedric (LeJuene) Thompson; John O. Parker III; Gregory (Marilyn) Allen; Carole Ellerbe–McDowell; Kevin Parks; Ray Watkins; Tri-State Reunion Choir; Dana L. Redd; Steve Hargrove; Yalonda Gambrell; Kelly Mobley; Chrystal Gains; Corrine's Restaurant; Pastor Richard Smith, Sr.; Dr. Ethan Ogletree; LeJuan Samuel; Dorce (Patricia) Hamilton; Robbin Russell family; Chris (Virlyn) Hamilton family; Ronald (Shirley) Russell family; Michael Hamilton family;

Dawn Russell family; Pastor Albert Morgan; Earnest Pugh; Tomar Jackson; Robin Carney–Britt; Chanel Overton; Renee Thomas; Kimberly (Greg, Julian, Mykal–Michelle) Harris family; LeShan Reid; Kanita Benson; Kellee Banks; Jack (Jeana) Harris family, The Diggs family (Suffolk, Virginia); The Viner family (Roanoke, Virginia); Brennen Pritchett; Vine Street; Alonzo Brooks; Donald Ashley; Marcus Witherspoon; Lisa R. Smith; Forbes; Mark Roberts; Rory (Keva, Antonia) Adams; Sherman Diggs III; Claneece Williams; Brandon Dutch; Doug Overton; Chris Collins – *Anointed News Journal*; Chris Schley; Terry (Felecia, Olivia) Truitt; Brian Williams; Austin Woodlin; Tameka Ferebee; Bishop Kenneth Moales, Jr.; Tyrone May, Jr.; Ronnie Dixon; Glenn Barrett; Craig Bauer; Jonathan DuBose; Francesca DeFrank; Malachi Macho; Al Edmundson; Caroline Drumgoole; Joel Bryant; Gabriel Hardeman; Edwin Hawkins; Bishop Marvin L. Winans; Chris Squire; Steven Ford; Chef Kendal Shelby; Bryne K. Price; Glenn Harvey DeVine; Troy Chambers; Patty Jackson; Elder Goldwire McLendon; Walter Stuart; Michael Roberts; Kevin Bond; Katherline Diggs–Wilson; Clarence "Nat" Williams; Kevin Travers; Tracy Diggs – Lash Diggs; Desiree Dezzie Neal; Kirsis Castillo; Pastor Patricia Cooper; Mike's Garage; Michael Edwards; David Bussie; Jessica Horne–Greene; Loren Dawson; Tye Tribbett; Candy West; Selesha Hawes; Jimmy – Pizza Express; iKenRock Entertainment; D'Garia Music Group; Young Black Successful; Called to Refresh; The Conversation; Staywoke; Cover Me Summit; L'NIS Senior Care; Third Base Trophy

Cover Photos: Kelly De'Anne Mobley

Cover Design Concept: Shavonya Jarman

COMMENTS

- Professor Diggs, Thank you for your hard work, creativity, and willingness to produce the best for God. —*Bishop David G. Evans, Bethany Baptist Church, Lindenwold, New Jersey*

- I've worked with Gary for over ten years, and in that time he has proven to be a great musician, songwriter, friend, and a true testament to how consistent hard work yields longevity in this industry. —*Derrick Hodge, Multi-Award Winning Music Producer, Seattle, Washington*

- There are many words I could use to describe Gary. Professional, courteous, spirit-filled, and highly skilled are just a few. However, I choose to use one word that sums it all up ..."phenomenal." —*Jamar Jones, Music Producer / Former Executive Music Minister – The Potter's House, Dallas, Texas*

- Gary is a great friend, brother, and a great asset to the industry. —Cedric Thompson, *Multi-Award Winning Music Producer, Charlotte, North Carolina*

- You can say Gary and I grew up together as young musicians making a name for ourselves in the Philly- and Jersey-area music scene. Our paths crossed many times at various churches, concerts, recording studios. I've always had mad respect for him, not only for his musical talent, but for the honorable man that he is. Much love to you my guy, continue to be blessed. — James Poyser, *Multi-Award Winning Music Producer, Philadelphia, Pennsylvania*

- Gary Diggs is not only an anointed minstrel of God, he also is a servant after the very heart of God. He plays, writes, produces, and worships under the very power of God and lives a life that shows forth God's glory!!! —*Benita Jones, Gospel Recording Artist, Atlanta, Georgia*

- Gary Diggs is a mentor and big brother of mine. Someone who I can call in the time of need for advice. I cherish the relationship we have beyond music because it has carried me through some rough sea- sons. —*Parris Bowens, Multi-Award Winning Music Producer, Willingboro, New Jersey*

- But when the man on the piano was playing, I don't know if people study Prophet postures. But I began to consume his in touchness and oneness with God. That's ok - He was so strategic, so methodical, so intentional. He plays on purpose. —*@BBCofNJ Impact Conf. 2019 Guest Speaker Prophet Todd Hall, Orlando, Florida*

- It has been my pleasure to work with Gary Diggs over the years. He is an incredibly talented producer and always a consummate professional to work with. — *Robin Crow, Owner of Dark Horse Studio, Franklin, Tennessee*

- Gary Diggs displays an intrinsic value for what is truly valuable in life, which is your faith and your family. His conversations are laced with pride and admiration towards both his God and his offspring. —*Shyami Maridjan, The Netherlands*

- I've known Gary for many years and apart from his amazing talent – I've always appreciated his heart to lead people into God's presence and help others who are called to worship ministry to do the same. —*Sam Towns, Worship Leader Hobart, Australia*

- Gary is more than a musician and technician. He is a leader in the industry of arts and has a authentic heart for worship. He is impeccable on his approach to define the word of God within worship. His expression of serving God includes the excellence of reaching God's heart and his people. —*Dr. Ethan Ogletree,*

New Destiny Praise and Worship Center, Houston, Texas

- Gary Diggs is a stand-up guy in a day and age where crooks are celebrated. It's great to have somebody who is the same in front of you and when you're nowhere around. His life and words have meaning. —*Richard Tubbs Smith, Jr., Music Producer, Egg Harbor, New Jersey*

- The character of a good friend is like a star. You don't always see them, but you know they're always there. That good friend is Gary Diggs. —*Vidal Davis, Multi-Award Winning Music Producer, Philadelphia, Pennsylvania*

- There are some people in life that will never know to what degree their influence catalyzed and shaped the lives of those around them. Gary continues to create platforms that allow people to discover new levels of greatness in themselves. For this he is my fondest mentor. —*Dana Sorey, Multi-Award Winning Music Producer, Wilmington, Delaware*

- Gary has been a friend and brother of mine for close to twenty-five years. He is a phenomenal top-tier musician, producer, songwriter and when you couple that with someone who is genuinely humble and unfathomably consistent, you have the incomparable

person of Gary Diggs —*Jamie Williams, Wall Street
Executive, Sicklerville, New Jersey*